Power in Pe

Jeff Grillo

978-0-9964750-0-6

2015

Power in Perseverance

Table of Contents

Guide

Power in Perseverance
Jeff Grillo

Author's Note:

G-d is Holy and cannot allow sin into his presence without it destroying us! By the way, this is not a typo. I deliberately removed the vowel from G-d. Why? Long story, but suffice it to say, it has to do with obeying the command to not desecrate the name. Also, I want everyone to read this. Orthodox Jewish people would stop reading immediately if they saw the vowel in there. So out of respect for the Word, and for my Jewish friends, I eliminate the vowel there.

Diminishing Sight

Part 1

The Problem that Produces Perseverance

CHAPTER ONE

My parents took me to Boston for some extensive eye examinations when I was about five years old. They decided to bring me to the Massachusetts Eye and Ear Infirmary because of a family history of blindness and certain signs that I began showing. A prominent doctor and researcher practiced there – a man named Elliot Berson. He was a specialist in Retinitis Pigmentosa; RP for short. In my case, this was a genetic retinal degeneration that results in the gradual loss of peripheral and low-light vision. This diminishing of sight usually continues until the sufferer is completely without sight. The most prominent RP sufferer is Stevie Wonder.

Years later, my parents sat down and broke the news to me that this was my lot in life. I had already known that I had a problem with my eyes. I knew that I wasn't like everyone else. I had trouble reading the blackboard at school. I was clumsy. There was rarely

4

a day that I was not tripping over things and knocking objects over. One could say I lived a "bull in a China shop" kind of existence. One of my earliest memories was of being a very little boy, riding in the backseat of my family's car at night and asking my dad how he knew where he was going. It seemed very scary to me – the prospect of driving at night. I mean, it is so dark. How could you know when or where to turn?

My parents told me that the doctors said that I would not be able to see much at all past the age of ten or eleven. I believe I was about that very age at the time of this discussion.

The intention of my parents was not to scare or depress me but rather to inform me so that I could best prepare for my future. They encouraged me to study hard in school, and as the Army used to say, "Be all that I could be."

Honestly, the details of my life concerning this subject of blindness could be a book in itself. Suffice it to say, that I am leaving much of the trauma and difficulty out for the sake of painting a broader picture for you at this point. I think that it would be safe for you to fill in the blanks with some of the apparent difficulties and challenges that most people would imagine.

I wish I could say that I took the advice of my mom and dad and went on to become an academic success. To say that was the case would be an awfully big fabrication. In fact, in my younger years, I believe that a sense of hopelessness took over. On the outside, most people would say that I was a good boy, a happy kid, and a funny and fun-loving child. The reality is that I think I used the façade to cover up the hopelessness I felt inside. I think my attitude towards school was more or less, "What's the point?" Everything I thought I would like to do, I felt as if I would be unable to do if I were to at some point become blind. Let's face it, vision is essential for such jobs as being a doctor, pilot, emergency worker, reporter, or soldier. Speaking of being a soldier, in high school, I talked to recruiters and was told by every branch of the military that I wouldn't pass basic training. I was even rejected by my own country!

A part of me has always felt that I was capable of so much more than what I was actually achieving. This posed a tremendous conflict in my mind. I began to battle within myself. The part of me that said, "Why try" began to grapple with the part of me that believed there was greatness down deep inside of me.

How could this be? How can I be great when I am disabled? The argument itself made no sense to me.

But still, I had that glimmer of hope that someday, somehow, I could become something more than what the stereotypical blind person could achieve.

After graduating high school in 1987, I received Yeshua HaMaschiach (Jesus the Christ) as my personal L-rd and Savior. My salvation and subsequent filling of the Holy Spirit began to water those tiny seeds of hope.

But before the seeds could germinate, something else in me had to die.

All through school, I was different from everybody else. Not different in the way you would want to be, but not as good as the other students, both academically and athletically. I had a hard time with school because of my eye problems.

I found it difficult to pay attention to what was being written on the blackboard. I had trouble keeping up with reading assignments. I tried to play it off as though I were the class clown rather than attempting to get help with my studies. I tried to act like I didn't care, and I tried to make fun of just about everything.

Sports were a joke; eye-to-hand coordination was pretty bad. Athletic prowess, or lack thereof, was a trademark for me. The best I could handle was joining the cycling club, a non-competitive social-type club. I

7

was also a ski club member, again more of a social organization than anything competitive.

I wanted to fit in like most kids growing up. I wanted to score the winning point in a big game. I wanted to stand out and be really good at something. Anything. Honestly, the only thing I was truly good at in all my years of school was surviving.

I can recall many occasions when I would leave a classroom to go to the bathroom and return to a dark room. The lights would be turned off, and the teacher would show a film strip or use the overhead projector. I would get scared knowing that I could not see in the dark. I was too embarrassed to ask for help or to show the class how "needy" I was. I would either skip the rest of class or otherwise roam the hallways and wait for class to end. Then, of course, I would have to face the music. I sometimes concocted stories about what had happened or where I had been. I rarely had the courage to tell the teacher in private what happened.

Driving for me was an absolute thrill. To me, driving represented a certain kind of freedom. I'm sure it means the same to most people. I was especially excited about motorcycles. I had always dreamed of having my own bike and cruising on the open highway. What a great thrill that would be! I did earn a license when I was finally old enough, but not without restrictions. My parents wisely took me to an eye specialist who examined me to be sure it was safe for me to drive. The doctor agreed that it would be alright then as long as I agreed to a "daylight operation only" license. My night vision was far too poor even to consider allowing it.

I took whatever I could get. However, it did pose many logistical nightmares for me along the way. I always had to know precisely what time it was, the weather conditions, how far from home I was, etc. Any miscalculation would have left me stranded. Keep in mind that this was before cellular phones were so commonplace. Even though they were around, they were far too large and expensive for a young adult.

In 1990, I somehow managed to get accepted into a college in Florida. I entered a Christian college as a music major. I was able to pass my classes, although barely, in some cases. Even with glasses, it was getting more difficult to read, but I managed. What was becoming even more difficult was reading and playing music. I learned to play the organ when I was 5 years old. Admittedly, I wasn't that good, especially for as long as I could play. I love to play very much; however, I could never play a song all the way through. I was unable to "sight read" at all. I would learn songs that I had heard and liked. Then, I'd get the sheet music and study it. I would usually learn the chords and then figure out the melody or some part of the song that I thought was cool. It just became too tedious for me, and I just couldn't do it. It was such a frustrating thing for me – to love something so much but to be utterly unable to do it.

I gave up on college after one year of struggling to get through it. I gave in to my frustrations and belief that I was "less than" – that I was somehow unable. Years later, I changed majors when I returned to college.

There were frustrations galore when it came to employment. I especially had a hard time seeing in low light. I had special troubles when I had an interview! Adapting from the bright outdoor light to "normal" office lighting was a huge challenge. In addition to the fact that I simply couldn't see well in low light, it was especially tough adjusting between extremes.

Consequently, I would look or at least feel foolish stumbling around the office. Filling out job applications became tougher and tougher as the years went on. My handwriting became sloppier as my vision diminished. It seemed the harder I tried to be neat when I wrote, the worse my handwriting got.

10

Most of the jobs I held were entry-level jobs. What else could I qualify for without a degree or experience anyway? My work was usually below par. I had many data entry jobs. My skills were good. I was very nimble and quick on a keyboard of any type. My eyes, however, were very show; therefore, my production almost always suffered. Again, I would try to cover up by making excuses or playing the clown. As a result, poverty became my dwelling place. Subsequently, if it weren't for my parents bailing me out often, I would have had much more difficult times. As it was, life was painfully difficult.

The ultimate sight-related job crisis came in 1996 when I landed my "dream job." I loved Boston radio. Growing up in Southeastern Massachusetts, we got all the great Boston radio stations. Being a top ten market, we had great talents on the radio, such as Sonny Joe white, Dale Dorman, Scott Robbins, and many others. I would sometimes dream of being as cool and smooth as they were. Naturally, I never even attempted to work in that industry because I had no training. I had some good friends and family that would tell me I had a great voice, and that I would be perfect in radio. My poor self-image never allowed me to take it seriously. Although, it made me feel good to hear the encouraging words.

Finally, out of frustration, I thought I'd try to get into radio so that I would hurry up and fail and be able to get everyone off of my back.

Through some other terrible circumstances, I found myself recounting a bad thing that had happened to me on a morning call-in show. I told the sad story in a rather funny exchange with the DJs. They aired the tape later in the program. Then, I went to the station to get a copy of the tape to play for my friends. While there, I met one of the morning DJs and asked him how people get started in radio. He told me that they usually began as interns. I asked him how you became an intern. He said, "You ask." So, I said, "Can I be an intern?" To which he replied, "You start Monday!" That is how I got started in radio!

Ten months later, I headed to Florida to return to school again. I was able to line up a job in the Tampa market. It was my first real gig, which got me on the air all by myself in a big market. The trouble came trying to be smooth and cool without sounding like I was reading! Unfortunately, it was essentially a liner format, meaning that almost everything I ever said on the air was scripted. I struggled so hard to make it. In the beginning, I sounded like a five-year-old reading "See Spot Run."

I found that to even have a chance at making it, I would have to painstakingly memorize every break before I went to air. This was the only way.

Believe it or not, I got to work with some great talent who tried hard to help me. Scott Robbins, whom I listened to growing up, was now my co-worker! He was a super guy who took a liking to me and would often encourage me. I also got to work with Rich Fields. He had been all over. He had been working in Los Angeles and had done television, too. When Rod Roddy passed away, Rich Fields became the new announcer for the Price is Right TV gameshow. Rich was also very helpful to me. He would offer help and advice whenever he could.

Despite working with great, talented people, I could not make it. Again, I felt on several different levels that my eyesight had cost me yet another opportunity.

I held a job long enough to get help from the Division of Blind Services. They helped me get training to become a Licensed Massage Therapist. I never in a million years thought for a second about doing this type of work, but I had come to a place in my life where I determined that there wasn't much else I could do. I mean, what else could a blind man do? I know plenty of people have overcome this handicap and have done great things with their lives, but the question remains: how could I? In my mind, the only good things about being a massage therapist were that I didn't need to have good or even any eyesight to do it, and I could earn a living. At least, I thought I could do better financially than what I had been doing.

I was now relying on adaptive technology more and more to survive. I needed a CCTV (closed circuit television) to read printed material. I also had a computer program called Zoom Text to see a computer screen.

My white cane also helped me be more independent. I resisted using it, though. I was ashamed to use it. I was deeply in denial. Using a cane to me meant that I was blind. I had minimal sight, but not enough to get around by myself a lot of the time. As such, I lost my driver's license due to my eyesight in 1999. The loss of my license meant the loss of my freedom. I felt an iron door had been slammed shut on me. It felt like a death of sorts. Years later, I still don't know if I can adequately tell what it meant to me to go through this experience.

I cried. It was one of the most challenging times of my life. I was so desperate for G-d to help me. Heal me. Anything! Science had nothing to offer. No hope. This disease was unstoppable, according to the medical community. Still, I believe that someday, somehow, I will see again.

My eyesight continued to diminish and caused me great anxiety until 2006. I completely depended on others to help me get around by this time. I still had some residual sight, but I often joked that I saw just enough to make me dangerous! Mainly, I thought I could see better than I actually could. I was still firmly stuck in denial. I refused to believe the doctors' report. I was refusing to believe, literally, what I could see. It seems the more I lost my sight, the more I started to call on G-d. I have always believed G-d heals. I had NO problem believing G-d could and would heal someone else. However, it was another thing to believe for myself. I almost started to think that somehow, G-d would use me "as is," but something deep inside of me cried out for total healing.

Now, at this time, the only way I could anything was with some sort of assistance. I had to either have someone read to me or use a CCTV. I refused to learn Braille. I still did not want to go all the way. I would not submit myself to the disease. I was not going down without a fight.

I was starting to use my cane a little more. I mainly used it when I was on my own and had to do things for myself, but I didn't like it. Things began to change for me in April of 2006 in a way only I could have imagined. I'll pick up on this part of my story in later chapters. By focusing on the suffering I endured up to this point in this section of my book, I feel you will appreciate the fullness of my testimony about the testing of my faith. Through tests, we become worthy of the prize waiting for us on the other side.

The Bible tells us that afflictions produce perseverance; perseverance produces character; character produces hope; and hope never fails (Romans 5:4).

I did not share these stories so that you may feel sorry for me. I did not share them so you will pat me on the back either. They are simply my story. Good or bad, it is what I went through. Ecclesiastes says that we "endure nothing, except that which is common to man." Whatever I went through is in no way unique. It may have felt that way, and believe me, it often did, but the fact remains that multitudes of people have gone through similar and even worse situations than I have.

The truth is that whatever you are going through right now, whether it is physical, emotional, financial, or spiritual, it may seem like all is falling apart around you, and nobody knows the trouble you've seen. I'm here to tell you that I am living proof that once you get through it, you will see clearly (no pun intended) that what you went through was no different than what countless souls have contended with throughout time.

You are not alone. We must each determine within ourselves that we will persevere to the end.

The Cancer

CHAPTER TWO

Life is anointed to frustrate you!

1992 was the year that the rug was pulled out from underneath me, and my eyes were opened to see just how extremely fragile this life is. I was exposed to a reality I had never really confronted before this time. I had become intimately aware of my own mortality. This came with the diagnosis everyone dreads, and it came to me at age 21.

I had completed my first year at Bible college and was embarking on a new chapter of my life. I was about to turn 21, and I took the semester off to get married. I was showering one day, and I noticed a tiny bump in one of my testicles. It was pretty small, but I had never noticed it before, and it was pretty tender to the touch. I had no idea what it could be.

I was pretty naïve at the time and not very medically savvy. I began to worry about all sorts of things it could be, but I don't think I ever considered the possibility of cancer.

I had been looking into getting health insurance but didn't have any at the time of this discovery. I worried about what to do about this bump. Several weeks went by, and still, I did nothing except worry. Mainly because I had no insurance. A big part of why I did nothing was because I was nervous and embarrassed. I mean, let's face it: the last thing I was interested in doing was walking into a stranger's office and asking the practitioner to inspect my genitalia.

Finally, the lump had grown to the point where the pain demanded attention. I could no longer wait and delay the inevitable. I was being forced by the pain to take action. It had gotten so bad that I could hardly walk.

Phone call after phone call to a number of doctors produced nothing. Without insurance, I couldn't even get a doctor to see me. In a panic, I kind of went a little nuts on one poor woman. I basically freaked out and asked what in the world I was supposed to do. Was I just supposed to lie down and die? What if this was serious? The woman directed me to the free clinic in town.

I was headed to the Judeo-Christian Clinic in Tampa. I was mortified on a few different levels. First, I was embarrassed that I had to have a stranger inspect areas that I was not interested in showing off. Second, I was embarrassed that I lacked insurance and the funds to get checked out.

Eventually, I got in to see a doctor at the free clinic. There was no way out of it. I had to drop my pants and allow this doctor to examine the lump that was causing me so much grief. Almost immediately, the doctor told me that it was definitely a tumor. He was quick to explain that, in most cases, they are benign and not to worry much about it. He made the recommendation for me to see a urologist. I was told that this particular doctor would see me and essentially donate his time and services to me. I was so blessed to get involved with the doctors that I did.

Once again, I found myself in the awkward position of having yet another stranger invade my modesty. Again, I was told it was a tumor and that more tests would be necessary to determine what should be done. I was sent for an ultrasound and nuclear diagnostic testing. There are many interesting aspects of these events that I will glaze over for the purpose of expediency.

Once all tests were performed, I sat in the waiting room and waited to get the "all clear," so I could leave. The technician who performed the tests came out and told me I was all set to go. The results of the tests would be passed along to my doctor, who would review them and contact me later. This was a Friday, and with the pain and anxiety I was feeling, I couldn't bear to wait a few more days. I pressed the technician for more information. I told her that surely she knew what she was looking at and asked her to please give me an idea of what was going on. It was then that, I am sure, she broke an ethical rule. She definitely stepped outside her scope of practice. I got what I asked for, but I assure you that I wasn't ready for it. She knelt down and grabbed my hand. She said, "Mr. Grillo, I'm afraid you're looking at the worst-case scenario."

A blackout is a phenomenon I had heard about in the past but couldn't fully understand. It was foreign to me and, quite frankly, sounded a bit nutty. However, when I heard the words "worst-case scenario," in my mind, it meant death. I believe I blacked out as soon as those words were spoken. I honestly do not remember being able to hear anything or see anything. Everything was dark and silent. I do remember having the overwhelming urge to scream, but I couldn't.

The next thing I remember, I was standing up in the middle of the waiting room. The technician and my fiancée were each holding onto me and trying to snap me out of it.

"Mr. Grillo….Mr. Grillo….Are you ok?" I came to, and told them I was fine. I thanked her for her time and told her to have a good weekend. I walked out of the hospital and headed towards my pickup truck. Once I

21

got into the truck, I lost it. The overwhelming feeling of despair took over my emotions. I began to cry uncontrollably. I cried out, "Why?" I pounded the interior door over and over. I thought I had just been given my death sentence. How could this happen to me? Why me? What did I do to deserve this? I'm only 21! I'm not ready to die!

It was truly the worst moment in my life. I had never been so scared in my life. Never since that time have I felt what I felt that day. I was a Christian. I am not sure why I reacted so desperately; the only explanation is that I knew in my spirit it wasn't my time. However, in light of the diagnosis, I could not stand too tall. My faith had never been tested too much before this time. I had so many lessons to learn, but despite my momentary outburst of emotions, I persevered.

I was not filled with courage. I confess I was scared to death through most of this ordeal. I held on firmly to my belief that, somehow, I would get through this. It was a tiny mustard seed-sized bit of faith, but I was clinging to that glimmer of hope. It was all I had.

I was called into the urologist's office to hear the results of my testing. He explained that all tests confirmed that it was definitely a tumor. There was no doubt. The only way to know for sure whether it was benign or malignant was to do a biopsy, which meant I had to have surgery. I had never been operated on in my life except for when I had my tonsils out when I was about five years old.

The day for surgery came. I was beyond terrified; they had to sedate me before they took me into the operating room. I was really worried that I wouldn't wake up. I was also worried that if I did wake up, what news would I be waking up to? I tried to calm myself and think positive, happy, good, Christian thoughts. I failed miserably.

The surgery was a success, and I recovered quickly. The biopsy not only showed that the tumor was malignant but that there were not one but two types of malignancy.

One tumor was a simple germ cell seminoma. It was malignant yet not terribly scary. The second tumor type was an embryonal carcinoma. This was an extremely malignant type of cancer. It is my understanding that it is considered so dangerously deadly because it spreads quickly. Truth be told, it has a 90% death rate because you don't know you have it until it is too late. Let that sink in for a few moments. The good news I learned was that it responds well to chemotherapy. The sole reason I found it early was because I was hemorrhaging into the tumor, which is what caused the pain. So to this very day, I say, "Thank G-d for hemorrhaging tumors!"

They had no choice but to remove the one testicle. The surgeons did some exploratory surgery and found no sign of spreading.

I was told to "thank my lucky stars," go home and get on with my life. It was highly recommended that I see an oncologist who would monitor me to ensure it didn't come back. That is exactly what I did, except it wasn't my "lucky stars" but G-d Almighty that I was thanking!

This whole thing started in August. I was diagnosed in September. My surgery was at the end of October. It was now December, and I was at my first meeting with the oncologist.

My oncologist was a young doctor named Dr. Rand Altermose. From what little I could see of him, he looked a bit like a mad scientist. His hairdo resembled Albert Einstein's. He also had a demented sense of humor, which I later came to love.

I was sent for a round of blood work and then came to his office for consultation and testing results. It was explained to me that according to the tests, I was either pregnant or had cancer somewhere in my body. This was the first of many weird attempts at humor that this man would make. Obviously, pregnancy was

24

not in the realm of possibilities, so we began to tackle the cause of the elevated blood markers.

Scans revealed that there were no detectable tumors anywhere. The blood markers told a different story. They showed that active cancer was on the move someplace.

Dr. Altemose gave me my options. He said we could go with "Plan A," which was to do nothing, and maybe I would survive one year without treatments. Then, there was "Plan B." "Plan B" was an aggressive combination of chemotherapy. He said it sounded scary, and quite frankly it was. However, he explained that despite the difficulties of treatment, I would have a much better chance of long-term survival due to the fact that it was caught very early.

I spent all of about ten seconds contemplating the choice. I told him, "That's not much of a choice. I'll take Plan B. He said, "I knew you'd see it my way."

Plans were immediately made for admission into St. Joseph's Cancer Institute in Tampa, Florida. The treatment plan called for 9 to 12 weeks of chemotherapy. The drugs would be administered in three week cycles. Week one would be as an inpatient in the hospital. From Monday through Friday, I would be connected to IVs that would give

25

me a constant supply of drugs, including cancer-fighting drugs, anti-nausea, pain medication, and fluids. Weeks two and three would consist of two outpatient visits to the hospital.

Reality differed only slightly. The outpatient weeks usually resulted in being readmitted to the hospital. This resulted from bad infections resulting from damaged immune responses from the chemotherapy. It was a very long and traumatic few months.

My first round of treatment came just before December 25th. I got out of the hospital just in time on the 2rth to have dinner with my family. My mother had made a nice traditional Italian meal, which included lasagna—one of my favorites. I was warned not to eat anything spicy or acidic because the chemotherapy would do damage to my stomach lining. Well, I felt pretty good, and I do love a good lasagna dish. So, I indulged just a little bit. A short time later, I paid the price.

It was the first of many scary moments. I ran to the bathroom and vomited. It was awful. In addition to the usual unpleasantries of that experience, I now had to endure added fear. Apparently, my body was becoming more sick and weak. I remembered my mother crying. I cannot even imagine what my mom and dad went through. Now that I have a child, I can only wonder at the fear and sense of helplessness they must have felt.

New Year's Eve was another stand-out moment for me. I was staying at the hospital that night. My parents came to visit me. I don't remember the time, but I do remember having the television on and being a little out of sorts during their visit. At one point, my mom came over and brushed my shoulder. She told me I had something on it. She then realized that I had several hairs all over my shoulder and pillow. "Oh, no!" I thought. I ran my hand through my hair, and large clumps came out into my hands. It was something I knew could and probably would happen, yet it still came as a shock and surprise.

I remember standing in the bathroom staring into the mirror when I got out of the hospital. I looked tired and not myself. The bald spots all over my head made me look downright weird. I remember speaking firmly to the mirror aloud, "Cancer, you aren't taking my hair…I AM!!!"

I refused to watch the progression of the treatments rob me of my physical identity. I grabbed a can of shaving cream and some razors and started shaving my head bald. It took a while because I had quite a thick head of hair.

I stood and stared into the mirror again once it was all off. Some tears were shed, partly out of sorrow for what I was dealing with but mostly for the small triumph, I had just leveled against the disease that had declared war on me.

One good thing about the head-shaving moment was that I discovered I had a pretty good-looking melon underneath all that hair! I no longer feared balding later in life. I even thought I almost looked cool!

It is difficult to summarize these months' events in one book chapter. This event alone could fill an entire book if I wanted to tell of every fear, every trip to the emergency room, every doubt, and every triumph. There were so many challenges; it is hard to pick a few to talk about without feeling like I am cheapening my experience.

In some ways, the experience was not quite as bad as I had imagined it would be. Never again, though, would I want to endure that fight again. I would not wish it on anyone, friend or foe.

Thank G-d Almighty that He allowed me to survive and tell the story. Thank G-d for helping me overcome this challenge in my life. Today, I am a different person in so many ways because I persevered through that trial. I would not be quite the same today if I hadn't been tested through the fire. I guess this is a shining example of what the Bible says in Romans 8:28, "All things work together for good, for those who love the L-rd, and are called according to His purposes." This is one event in my life that Satan meant for harm, but G-d turned it around in the end and used it for His Glory.

G-d was merciful to me. The 9 to 12 weeks turned out to be eight weeks. The doctors came to me with the good news in the seventh week. All blood markers were now in the normal ranges. I was given the option to stop treatments or to continue one more week just to make sure it was all gone. The doctor recommended the latter, and I agreed. What was one more week of suffering? I certainly didn't want to leave any room for having to deal with this again later. So, we pressed on for one more week.

For one year, I would have to go for monthly bloodwork to monitor my blood and be ready to attack again should anything look abnormal. It was a hard year. The anticipation of each upcoming test was followed by worrying about the possible outcomes. Even after I had my tests done, I had to endure the agony of waiting for the results, which sometimes took several days. Each test came back in my favor. After the first year, I came once every six months, and now I still go once a year.

It has now been 14 years since my last treatment. Doctors consider one cured after 5 years. It is purely academic at this point. I've been told that there simply aren't many survivors of this type of cancer after such a long period. All the credit goes to Jehovah Rapha, the L-rd, my Healer.

Today, I still cannot help being a little anxious when health concerns arise. I regularly went to the doctor after treatments were over. I would go in there nervous about a bump on my back. The doctor would examine me and tell me that he thought I would survive this one..."It looks like a pimple." He told me that all of us cancer survivors were all the same – a bunch of chickens! I guess that may be so, considering what we have gone through. Is it any wonder?

Cardiac Scare

CHAPTER THREE

Fear is a paralyzing power that will block your faith.

My family has not exactly been blessed with the best cardiovascular health known to man. My dad told me of family members who had died young from heart attacks. He tried to warn me so I could do things to prevent myself from traveling down that same road. It was in September of 1990 when the unthinkable happened to my dad.

One afternoon, I visited my parents with my roommate and his girlfriend. We had dinner- an Italian feast of pasta and meatballs. After dinner, Dad left the room. We continued talking with my mom for a while, and then she left to go check on my dad. She returned to tell us that he was lying down because he wasn't feeling well. I told her to give him a hug for me and tell him we said goodbye because we were going to head back to school.

The next morning, someone came running towards me as I walked across campus. They asked if I was Jeff Grillo. "Yes," I said. They told me that my mother had contacted the school. There was an emergency, and I should call her right away. I did just that. I was very nervous about what the news might be. I had never got a call like that from her before.

Mom was obviously upset, buy trying to sound strong on the phone, so she wouldn't cause me to panic. She told me that dad was really not doing well. He looked bad but was telling her he just had indigestion. He told her not to call 911. Thank G-d, Momma knew best!

She went off on her own and called for an ambulance. Mom requested that they not use their sirens when coming into the neighborhood so they wouldn't upset him. They honored her request and came quickly. They immediately assessed my dad and determined that he was having a mild heart attack. They took him to the hospital at once.

The next morning, the cardiologist entered his room just as my dad started to have a massive heart attack. They say that timing is everything, and it was perfect timing for sure in this case. The doctors said that if my dad had had this heart attack anywhere but in the presence of the doctor, he would have surely died. Some may call it lucky; we call it miraculous.

My dad had a quadruple bypass surgery to enable his heart to work properly. They told him that the bypass would be good for approximately seven years. I am excited to report that at the time of the writing of this book, he is alive and well some fifteen years later. It is one more manifestation of G-d's healing power and grace.

My cardiac troubles were discovered after gaining quite a lot of weight as a result of the drugs that had been administered to me during my chemotherapy. I weighed somewhere around 190 pounds at the start of treatment. I had ballooned to a whopping 245 pounds by the end of my treatments. The steroids they used to stimulate my appetite worked too well. Before treatment, I had an amazing, stable metabolism. Regardless of how I ate or whether or not I exercised, my weight remained constant. I'm sure my age had something to do with it as well. After therapy, my metabolism leveled off once again, this time at a much higher weight.

The weight problem began to take a toll on me. I had trouble climbing stairs without getting winded. I even began having chest pain. Sometimes, the chest pain would be rather bad. Naturally, in light of my family history, I began to worry greatly. I made an appointment with my dad's cardiologist. I had a number of tests done, and it was determined that I had trouble with one of my heart valves. They called it mitral valve prolapse.

My heart was weak, and instead of holding tight when it contracted, it buckled back into the upper chamber. This buckling put pressure on that valve and caused pain.

The doctor wasn't ready to do anything about it. Drugs were not really an option at that point, and surgery was an extreme that nobody wanted. The doctor told me that I had come too far and survived too much with cancer to end up dying from something stupid like a heart attack. I was told that with diet, and especially aerobic exercise, the heart would strengthen and eventually correct itself.

It was a scary time. Nobody wants to know that their heart has any kind of problem. It was unsettling news; however, the fact that it was within my control to correct it was somewhat comforting and liberating.

There were many scares, many trips to the emergency room at the local hospital, and there were many EKGs that followed over the years. I had trouble disciplining myself to do what was necessary, and I paid the price. Now, after many years, I have arrived at a place where I no longer have chest pains that once plagued me so often. I recently had testing done for my heart for other reasons, and the cardiologist found no sign of mitral valve prolapse! I still struggle with my weight, but I have lost and kept off over twenty pounds. My wife and I recently recommitted ourselves to improving our bodies. We are doing it both for our health and, yes, a bit for vanity as well.

I continue to make improvements, and I fully expect to be well under 210 pounds by the time this book is published. My ultimate goal is to maintain between 200 and 205 pounds.

The lesson I learned in all of this was again how immensely fragile life is. The Bible says we are fearfully and wonderfully made. We are complex machines, but simple things, like changes in our eating habits, can go a long way in determining our longevity.

I have made incremental changes in my life that, when they all add up, are leading me to a healthier and better life. Simple things like gradually adding exercise to my day, adding raw fruits and vegetables to my daily snacks, and making healthier choices can make a big difference. I've chosen whole wheat instead of processed white flour, olive oil instead of hydrogenated oils, and supplementing my diet with Omega-3 fatty acids. They all contribute to a healthier me.

The Anxiety Attacks Begin

CHAPTER FOUR

"For G-d has not given us a spirit of fear, but of power, and love and of a sound mind." 2 Timothy 1:7

Anxiety, to me, always seemed like something that other people had. More specifically, I had always pictured a nervous old woman when I thought of anxiety sufferers. That couldn't be further from the truth. Anxiety troubles all races, age groups, and most people. The difference is that for some people, it is nothing more than a passing anxious thought that is quickly dealt with and put under subjection. For others, including myself, it can be something much more sinister. The first time I recall having an "episode" came after my cancer experience. Satan used the fear instilled from that experience to fuel the next attack.

I remember how it first hit me. The first time is also how it usually comes. I usually mind my own business and do not think of anything particularly stressful when a flood of panic overtakes me out of nowhere. At one instant, it would feel like a brick wall had fallen on me. Literally, I would gasp. I found myself with the overwhelming realization that I exist in mortal flesh. Cancer has shown me how extremely fragile life is.

We are all precariously positioned in this life. Our existence is teetering between two worlds. We walk a tightrope every day, every moment, in fact. We live and move and exist in the current realm. The greater reality is that there is a razor-thin line we walk on, that at any moment, for any reason, we can find ourselves in the presence of the Almighty Living G-d in an instant. Even under the best circumstances (being a saved, born-again Christian), that is still an amazingly overwhelming prospect, even to me.

That moment in time will come without a shred of doubt for every person who has ever existed. The timing in which we meet the Creator is different for all of us, but the certainty of that destined meeting is set in stone. The only question is whether we are meeting Him for our reward and welcomed into eternal glory or we are meeting Him for our judgment and eternal damnation.

Fifteen years have come and gone since my experience with cancer. For nearly fifteen years, I have dealt with this attack from anxiety.

The Word tells us, "Fear of the L-rd is the beginning of wisdom." I still am not totally sure how much fear of the L-rd is healthy and at what point it becomes unhealthy. That is for another man of G-d or a mental health expert to determine; I can only share my experiences.

There is a good side to the plague of anxiety and fear of the L-rd to me. It has kept me in a place of reliance upon Him. I guess it is a blessing of sorts to have such a sober understanding of how terrifically awesome the L-rd G-d is and how small and helpless we are in comparison. I believe that is a good thing. Somewhere along the line, it spread into other areas of my life, and it became a somewhat debilitating condition that kept me from living a full life.

I can't recall the last time I had a specific moment of anxiety with respect to the fear of g-d or death at this moment. More recently, waves of panic have sprung up out of nowhere, with no specific cause that I could point my finger at. Stress, in general, is a contributing factor, so I've been told. In my case, I believe it to be true. Everyone has their own way of dealing with different types of stress. I am not terribly good at handling it sometimes.

Anxiety attacks come with a cascade of ill effects. First, there will be a drowning wave of panic. There is a heightened awareness of things like breathing and the ability to notice or hear my own heartbeat. My heart will tend to pound more and more furiously. My blood pressure will rise in tune with that increased pounding, sometimes even dangerously so. The panic will cause the otherwise natural release of adrenaline into the bloodstream. This increase in adrenaline levels causes the heart to race faster and faster. Blood pressure continues to rise. The desire to curl up into a ball and scream rises. This causes more panic, which in turn results in more adrenaline. You can see this is an awful and vicious cycle that feeds upon itself.

I haven't kept count over the years, but I'd say that panic attacks have sent me to the hospital more than cancer ever did. There were two separate periods in my life where it affected my life so profoundly that I had no choice but to go on medication to help regulate my brain chemicals. There were some side effects that I did not like, but it was much better than living with the dread that came from this condition.

Anxiety has kept me from normal activities in many different ways. I have not been able to even consider flying on a commercial airplane since 1999. The though of having a panic attack on a flight is too horrifying to me. I imagine I'd have to be tasered by the onboard marshal if I did have a panic attack on a flight! There have also been times when I did not go to social events because of fear. I avoid crowds at malls and other such places because all that commotion tends to set off an attack for some reason. It has even kept me from pursuing what G-d has planned for my life.

I was recently placed on medication for panic once again. I was told I would have to stay on it for at least six to nine months. After about two months, I determined that I would never take nor need to take this medicine again as long as I shall live. I am standing firm on the scripture I started this chapter with. So far, things are going well. I say that scripture out loud with authority if I feel something coming on. The feelings subside; they have to. How can it stand when confronted with the authority and power that is in the blood of Jesus? The law of displacement holds true. Only one thing can occupy a space at one time. I fill myself with the Word of God when I feel the enemy creeping in with a blanket of panic. I fell myself with the Spirit of G-d. All else must flee. So it says in His Word.

Financial Suffering

CHAPTER FIVE

"But my G-d shall supply all your need according to His riches in glory by Christ Jesus." Philippians 4:19 (KJV)

This may turn out to be the most difficult chapter to write in this book. It is not because of any shame or unwillingness to be candid when sharing my story, but rather just deciding where to begin. When in doubt, start at the beginning.

I grew up in a good family. My parents loved both my sister and me very much. My parents both worked very hard to provide a nice lifestyle. Dad held a very good paying job. Mom was a stay-at-home mom. She went back to work once my sister and I were old enough to take care of ourselves, but even then she was home by the time school let out most of the time.

My mom grew up in a rather financially poor family. She used to tell me stories about how she had to turn in every paycheck to her dad to help make ends meet. Then, she would get a little spending money for her trouble. I am certain it was because of that upbringing that she adopted a polar extreme when dealing with ther children. My mom helped me open a bank account when I was old enough to work, but she never really taught me how to manage money. She and my dad held the opinion that if we worked to earn money, then it was totally up to us what we did with that money.

As a teenager, that was a great deal! I mean, let's not fool ourselves, back then minimum wage was $3.35 per hour. The money I was able to rake in wasn't exactly impressive. What was impressive was how many ways I could find to blow my money. I quickly got into debt once I was old enough to drive. I borrowed money to buy a car and a motorcycle. I am not sure, but my total debt at that age ever really exceeded one thousand dollars, but at $3.35 per hour it was quite a hill to climb.

I would spend all kinds of money on food. This was ridiculous. There was always plenty of good food available home, but I loved to go out and waste money for some reason. My well-earned money would be spent on food, clothing, vehicle payments, gas and maintenance, music, electronic keyboard, movies, and much more. There was always something to pour my money into. I never considered saving my money. Minimum balance was my middle name.

My parents didn't realize it, and I'm very positive they never intended it, but they unwittingly set me up with a poverty mindset. There was never enough. I never learned to save. I never learned to tithe. I never learned to sow a financial seed.

Things only got worse as I got older. I really got hooked in the poverty loop when I was ready to start college. This time I was aided and abetted by an aunt. I was living in Massachusetts at the time, and I was "entitled" to help from the state due to my vision impairment. I was "entitled" to help with tuition. I was probably even "entitled" to draw disability income. It was my right. Our family paid taxes; therefore, there is no shame in taking back what belongs to me. Wow! That is quite the trap to get pulled into, and I got pulled in hook, line, and sinker.

I got accepted into a school in Florida. The blind services of Massachusetts were paying for basically all my school expenses. I had a brand new car by this time. It was a shiny new Ford for just under $10,000. I found myself a full-time student with no real expenses, other than a vehicle and related expenses. How perfect, right? Wrong. The poverty mentality got further twisted in my wrong-thinking mind.

I started thinking, which back then was quite dangerous. I decided that a visually impaired person needed to focus on studying, not working or worrying about being able to get to and from work. After all, I could not drive after dark, so how could I work anyway?

So, I did the natural thing that any wrong-thinking person would do. I decided that my disability money wasn't enough to support me, even though it probably was, and I began taking student loans to give me further a lifestyle that I thought I was "entitled" to have.

I thought, "Hey, once I graduate and get a good job, paying all this back will not be a problem." Wow, what a curse I was living under! To further complicate things, keep in mind I was going to a Christian college, yet I had never learned to be a faithful tither.

I found myself $30,000 in debt with no degree when all was said and done.

There were countless situations that I found myself stuck in along the way. Mom and Dad were always there to bail me out. Occasionally, I would have to pay them back, but they would usually look the other way and forgive the debt early. These were misguided acts of love. I appreciated each time they bailed me out, but the sad truth is that I never learned my lesson. In retrospect, the best thing they could have done was let me hang out to dry. Let me struggle and figure out my own mess instead of prolonging the madness.

I have to add a side note here. I do not hold my parents at all responsible for any of my financial troubles. I am merely telling things as I saw them happen. The reality is that I always made choices. It was my choices that got me into trouble. I take full responsibility for all that has happened to me. I probably could have turned a corner much earlier in life if I had sought good financial counsel. Unfortunately, I did not do that.

Now, I worked a radio job, making a whopping $9.00 per hour. One day, I finally realized that I had no way out. I was going deeper into debt every month. I had nothing to show for all my debt. I was in a truly shameful situation. It was my entire fault.

I remembered praying desperately to G-d that He would bail me out. My mom was no longer alive, and my dad wasn't able to bail me out any longer. Maybe G-d could bail me out now.

Somewhere, I learned that withholding the tithe from G-d equals robbing G-d (Malachi 3:8, 3:10, Haggai 1:5-9). How could I possibly expect G-d to hear my prayers and then bless me when I was robbing Him? It did not add up.

How in the world could I give ten percent of my horrible little income to G-d, or anyone, when I couldn't even make it on one hundred percent? I agonized over this for a long time. I read in the Bible that G-d says to test Him in this matter and see that He is good. Someone also told me that you cannot out-give G-d. Out of nothing more than pure desperation, I gave my entire next paycheck. I gave it all to G-d. "Here you go, G-d. Take the whole thing. Now show me something. You said to test You, so here's Your test." Looking back, I see that this was not the right attitude. However, I believed that G-d would either show me something miraculous or nothing much would change. I would never go back to my old way if G-d showed up, or I would have the green light to go my own way and forget about all this tithing business if it failed.

I can't explain what happened next other than to say that G-d showed up in a big way!

For the first time, there was enough. I'm not kidding. I even had a little extra at first. I got more hours at work. I got a raise shortly afterward. The money came in from sources I didn't expect. G-d gave me a wife. The wife He chose for me was exactly what I needed in so many ways. She had her financial act together. I tried to talk her out of marrying me. I didn't want her ever to think I married her for money or to "help me out" in any way. She understood exactly where I was and where I wanted to go and married me anyway.

In a little over five years, G-d took me from a huge debt, little or no money, and nothing to show for my work and brought me to a miraculous new place in my life. I finished training as a massage therapist. I then left the radio business and went into massage therapy full-time. I finally broke the curse of social welfare. I no longer accepted monthly assistance from the federal government. I no longer accepted Medicare health insurance. I worked super hard to earn as much money as I could. I continued tithing; I continued sowing financial seed and continued to reap the harvest. This is my testimony.

I got a new job as a therapist, which enabled me to make great money and have the opportunity for overtime. For the first time, my wife and I were building a new home just outside of Tampa. We stood on that land before the home was built, and I prophesied. I spoke aloud that somehow, within two years, this home would be paid in full. That statement sounded like pure craziness at the time. But guess what? G-d is faithful!

Just over two years later, property values doubled, and we sold that home and made a six-figure profit. We used it to buy a larger home with much more property in North Carolina for HALF the mortgage we had in Florida. Now, for the first time, my wife could stay home and be a full-time mom to our two-year-old son. G-d answered so many prayers for us. G-d is able to do exceedingly above all that we could hope, dream, or ask. Amen!

Disclaimer: I do not support or believe in the prosperity gospel nonsense. The crux of the prosperity gospel is that people are encouraged to give to receive a blessing. In other words, the treasure at the end is the focus and motivation, whereas a correct interpretation is that because we are blessed, we give out of a heart of gratitude, an offering that we may draw near to the Father. Not as some sort of an enticement to some Pagan deity to curry favor.   Our G-d is not a magic genie in a bottle that you can rub and manipulate. I believe in keeping His commandments to the best of my ability. I believe in His blessings and His curses as outlined in His Word.

The bottom line of this part of my story is this: learn to tithe, give above and beyond the title, and be a doer of His Word rather than a hearer only.

I don't think about money nearly as much now that I have some compared to when I had none. With all due respect to those who say having money is evil or not G-d's will, I say that type of thinking is a bit off base. Money is a tool for good or for evil. It's all you can think about when you don't have it. You think about it because you like to do things like eat, have a place to live, etc.

It is G-d's will to bless us. G-d made a covenant with Abraham, and if we are in Yeshua, we are heirs to all those blessings that G-d promised him. Today, we are giving like never before. I have learned that Jehovah Jirah is my provider. It is not my job. G-d never intended our jobs to provide for us. Our jobs are intended to put resources into our hands so that we may be a blessing to the Kingdom. The Israelites wandered in the desert for forty years! G-d met their daily needs along the way. He will be faithful in meeting all of our needs, too.

If you are not a tither and a giver, then pray about it and test G-d with a repentant heart. You will never regret it for a moment. I promise!

Living in "Denial" Can Be a Good Thing

Part II

The Product of Perseverance

CHAPTER SIX

Undoubtedly, you have heard the accusatory statement, "You're in denial!" In the past, I had always seen denial as a tool we use to help us ignore reality. Usually, this is a bad thing. For example, a husband thinks he has the perfect family when the reality is that he hardly spends time with his wife and children, and they strongly resent him. Perhaps acknowledging the reality of his struggling relationship with his family would be too painful for him because it would involve admissions he doesn't want to make and efforts he is not willing to expend. This would certainly be an example of denial in a negative sense.

Until recently, this is really the only way I have ever viewed denial. If a person was in denial, he or she avoided a painful reality. Avoiding their reality was a defense mechanism that was, in truth, counterproductive.

I have spent most of my life living deep in denial with regard to my visual impairment. I believed that I was somehow doing myself a disservice. Part of me thought that maybe I should just give in to the "reality" and direct my energies into constructive ways to deal with and overcome my loss.

I have consistently refused to do the logical things you would expect a person who is losing their eyesight to do. I refused to learn Braille, even though there have been numerous situations where it would have been an amazing asset and blessing to know how to read Braille. Learning Braille was an admission of sorts that the obvious was happening. A guide dog would have been a wonderful asset to me many times in my life, but I skillfully avoided getting involved in the necessary processes to get a dog. I rationalized my reluctance simply as a "need" issue. I said that there were many people far worse off than me who needed a guide dog. I turned it into an act of kindness in my own mind.

Let us not forget the white cane. Somehow, the use of the dreaded white cane was making me seem even more helpless than the use of a dog. At least the thought of having a guide dog had benefits beyond the obvious. Who wouldn't love having a beautiful, wonderfully trained, intelligent dog as a new best friend? How cool would that be, on at least that one level?

Eventually, I gave in, at least partially. I finally acquired a cane out of bare necessity when I lost my driver's license in 1999. I humbled myself enough to get it and learn the best way to use it, but that was about where it ended for a long time. The fact that I had some residual sight made the use of the cane all the more painful to me on so many occasions. The pain came from seeing people looking at me as I tapped along. Some gave looks of pity. Some looked on with simple curiosity. I hated being on display like that. I understand that the reality is that far fewer people noticed me in a negative way than I felt like they did. Knowing that in my head never really made it to knowing it in my heart. I may have had a weird combination of superiority and inferiority complexes simultaneously. Inferiority came from the obvious-feeling less than everyone around me. Superiority feelings were probably almost more delusional at times. I felt in my heart I was better than this. I felt so helpless and dependent; I felt capable of so much more in my heart of hearts. I felt like I wasn't handicapped. I never saw myself as disabled. Except for the blind thing, I was just like everyone else. How ridiculous was that?

I never felt like I was better than anyone else with a similar or even different disability. My feelings of superiority were honestly confined within myself. When I would tell myself I was better than that, it simply meant that I would not accept that level of standard for me.

I have always had the deepest respect and compassion for all people who have to deal with unwanted circumstances in their lives- whether that refers to a physical or mental problem or a situational challenge in their lives.

After some 36 years in this world, I have realized that denial is actually a good thing. Perhaps I should say denial "can" be a good thing. My decision to deny association with what life had dealt me gave me the ability to live above it in my mind. I was creating a reality in my mind that was different from the reality everyone else around me could see. All realities are conceived in the realm of the mind.

You must first conceive an idea or concept to create anything. Let's say you have a handicap that you are not thrilled with. You must first have the idea in your mind that the situation is unacceptable to you in order to make any change. You will never search for a solution until you first decide in your mind that your situation is unacceptable. Once that decision is made, you can search and find a way to correct it.

Medicine was failing me miserably. Science had no solution. That meant that the only other way was for me to receive healing from the only source left- G-d. I am in no way suggesting that G-d should be the last stop in your healing search. He should be the first. For me, it was almost simultaneous. I prayed and searched. I believe G-d uses doctors to do His work just as much as speaking a word.

So, in my case, my denial was my first step in the healing process. In my mind, I refused to accept what was happening to me. I was forced to look for an alternative by not giving in to the disease process. The only alternative for me was complete and total healing.

Satan is a liar. Not only that, but the Bible also says that Satan is the father of lies. The lie that I was blind and diseased was planted and cultivated in my mind. Denial was the tool I used to begin to get things turned around.

I denied the lie.

In my humble opinion, accepting your lot in life when it comes to handicaps is basically agreeing to sign your death warrant. If you are diagnosed as blind, and you agree to accept the diagnosis, forget it; you just signed the death sentence with regard to your vision. It will be lost. If you became paralyzed somehow and accept your new lot in life, again, you have sentenced your hope of healing to death. The same would apply to any unwanted condition: deafness, mental illness, MS, MD, or cancer. You name it; it all fits.

Denial isn't always an easy thing, but it is, in my opinion, the right thing. Challenge yourself today to begin your own denial mindset. If your troubles are financial, live in financial denial. Deny the lack in your life. Count your blessings (yes, you have them even in the face of adversity). Deny the spirit of lack. Deny the "reality" that you see and proclaim the "reality" you want to see. Denial is the tool that will take you from the reality of lack to the reality of abundance in this situation. If your trouble is in the area of a physical handicap or other shortcoming, deny it! Deny the "reality" you think you perceive and proclaim by asking G-d to help you achieve the reality you want. Persevere through your problems. The fuel for perseverance combines one part denial and one part proclamation. Deny what you do not want and proclaim while working toward what you do want. To deny troubles you have without the proclamation is problematic. That is a negative type of denial, a defeatist attitude. Remember, you cannot fix a problem that you do not think exists. Denial in this context is not the same. You see and recognize the trouble; then, you choose to deny it. You choose not to give it any power over you. That is where good denial comes from. Always remember to follow up with a proclamation.

There is power in denial; just be sure to use it for good!

Your Mind Is Your World!

CHAPTER SEVEN

So many books on the market tout the virtues of positive thinking. They teach you how to think and how to dream. I am humbled even to have the opportunity to add my brief perspective to the literary volumes of information on this topic. I am excited to share what I have learned about the power we have in our minds (our thinking) and in our tongues.

"As water reflects the face, so a man's heart reflects the man." Proverbs 27:19

"Such as a man thinketh in his heart, so is he." Proverbs 23:7

Nothing is greater than G-d's eternal Word. He often uses people to further His message. As such, there have been some non-biblical quotes that I consider some of my favorites. I wish I could claim I said them. Unfortunately, they are not my brilliant lines. I don't even know exactly who said them first, but I can tell you it was by people wiser than me.

"If you think you can, you're right. If you think you can't, you're right, too."

"What you can conceive and believe, you can achieve."

"You become like your most prevalent thought."

Our minds are wonderful, amazing biological machines. Our minds are complex. It is almost incomprehensible how fast and powerful they are. You sometimes hear people say, or perhaps you've said it yourself, that my mind is going a thousand miles per hour. Our minds are orchestrating countless functions and innumerable calculations per second, twenty-four hours a day, and seven days per week. We have eleven systems of the body, two hundred and six bones, over six hundred muscles, countless cells, and miles upon miles of blood vessels. All of this, each minute function and each interaction, is ultimately orchestrated by the brain. Science tells us we only use ten percent of our brain's capacity. There is great power in our minds.

We set new realities in motion by thinking a thought. Thoughts grow and become actions. Thoughts also cause the tongue and mouth to speak. We are told in Scripture that we have the power of life and death, blessings and curses in our tongues.

How did G-d create the universe and all that has ever been created? Did the omnipotent King of Kings get a pail, add all sorts of ingredients, mix it all up, and toss the bucket into eternity in order to spread His creation throughout space and time? No!! Did He get a hammer and nails and then start physically building things? No, absolutely not! Then how did He create the universe? The Word of G-d tells us that G-d spoke. All that was crated was done so by the power of the spoken Word of the L-rd.

What powerful stuff!

Consider this: we are created in G-d's image. We learn this in the book of Genesis. What does it mean to be created in His image? Does it simply mean we "look alike"? Does it refer to our basic human form? Is it speaking about our DNA? Is there something in that? What are we to make of this "image" stuff? I'll tell you what: image is everything! I believe all of the above is true.

Here's another concept submitted for your consideration. We are told that, "…the same Spirit that raised Christ from the dead dwells in us…" (Romans 8:11). Jesus performed amazing signs and wonders and healed all who were oppressed by the devil. He told the disciples that they would do these things and greater. If it is true that we are created in the image of G-d, that the Spirit dwells in us and that according to Christ we can do what He did; isn't it safe to draw the conclusion that what we speak can create or destroy, just as G-d does?

G-d is supreme, and the creation can never surpass or even approach the Creator. You can be certain that I am not having some prideful, satanic delusion that we can be as G-d. I am saying that G-d has given us the power and authority to do many wonderful things. The problem is that most of us either don't realize the truth, use the truth selfishly, or simply don't "get it." I didn't get it for 36 years! I heard about the power of our words an enormous amount of times. It never sank in, and I never truly grasped the magnitude of what it really and truly meant until recently.

This startling revelation has changed my life. The single most influential change that ever occurred in my life was the realization that I was a sinner and in need of a Savior. The greatest change in my life was when I accepted Yeshua HaMashiach (Jesus the Christ) as my personal L-rd and Savior. Second, the next greatest revelation in my life is understanding our words' impact. Our words can impact our lives and our realities. They affect our health; they affect our wealth. They affect people we love for better or worse. They affect everyone we speak to or about. It's almost scary how much power we have and what little thought we put into our chosen words. If we are to imitate our L-rd, it isn't any wonder then that scripture records that G-d's Word is "...alive and active. Sharper than any two-edged sword. It penetrates even to dividing soul and spirit, joints and marrow; it judges the thoughts and attitudes of the heart." The saying "whatever we conceive and believe, we can achieve" has a much deeper meaning in the light of who we are in Christ Jesus.

We can accomplish whatever our minds dream if we believe in our hearts, align ourselves with His will, and do not doubt.

I encourage you to take the time to get a concordance and look up all the scriptures related to thoughts and speaking. A wealth of knowledge is waiting for you if you seek it out. Plenty of books, even by Christian authors, explain at length how thoughts create action. You can change your future simply by changing your mind.

Pay attention to the words you say during the day. Listen to the words you hear others use. It will amaze you how easily we all toss around both heavy-duty blessings and curses without even realizing it. Unfortunately, you will probably find more curses than blessings.

Once you are able to detect these sometimes subtle parts of your speech, it will change you forever. You can take action once you recognize it in your own life. Guard your mind and your tongue. Be careful to stop the use of negative speech. Put a stop to the use of curses. Begin to speak life to everyone. Speak life to yourself.

If you have financial troubles, get your checkbook and speak life and abundance to it. If you are having marital trouble, get with your spouse and together agree, and speak life and health to that marriage. Tell your spouse every day how beautiful or handsome he or she is. Tell him or her how smart and important he or she is to you and the family and how precious he or she is to G-d. Even if it doesn't feel 100% true at first, in time, it will be! If your trouble takes the form of a vehicle with mechanical troubles that you cannot afford to fix, speak life into that car. Declare in the heavens that your car is sufficient to meet your needs. Then, speak to your job, and call into existence favor and promotion. Sow seeds of promise and life. Eventually, seeds always bring a harvest. Practice thinking, speaking, and becoming what you know G-d wants you to become.

Get the phrase "I can't" out of your lexicon of sayings. Remember, the Bible says, "I can do ALL things through Christ who gives me strength." Philippians 4:13

Our words can bring good or evil, just like seeds we sow can bring either good or bad harvests. Choose the good! Do not let yourself be tempted into saying the wrong things. We WILL be accountable for every idle word.

The Battle for Peace

CHAPTER EIGHT

"For G-d has not given us a spirit of fear, but of power, love, and of a sound mind." 2 Timothy 1:7

"…the peace that passes all understanding…"

I'm going to do something nutty. I will give you the whole point of this chapter right up front. I trust you will still read the rest of the chapter. I feel moved to get this out quickly and then expand on it further. It is so important that I want you to get this point above everything else in this chapter.

Perfect peace can only come after our submission and yield to G-d's perfect will.

I hope you get this point beyond the inspiring stories I share about situations and circumstances I have had to persevere through.

I have struggled throughout my life to discover who I am. I know this is the same thing we all go through.

I always believed I was somebody. I always believed I mattered. I always believed somewhere deep down in my heart that I would be something big. Of course, that "something" took many forms through the years. There were times I believed I would be a great rock star. I believed, or at least wanted to believe, that I could be an important political leader. I dreamed that I could be a great writer or actor. I had so many ideas of how greatness might come that I really never could stay excited about any one thing long enough to be focused on achieving it.

It is strange to say that I knew I was created for greatness because I had never successfully moved towards any of these lofty hopes in all my years. This created great turmoil inside of me. I have laid awake so many sleepless nights, struggling within myself to understand who I am and who I was to be. All I knew was that I was created for so much more than I lived up to. How would I ever amount to anything? I had so many obstacles to overcome. At least for a long time, I felt that I had so much more to overcome than everyone around me.

Other people had it easy compared to me, but I pressed on rather than give up or submit to my weaknesses and settle for an average life. This is the value of perseverance. You never know when it will pay off. Your troubles are only for a season. Your "shortcomings" are placed in your life strategically to position you for G-d's glory and greatness. The test is to see if we can be patient enough to wait, strong enough to continue in the face of adversity, and loyal enough to give G-d the credit for bringing you there once you have arrived.

G-d will not allow us to take more than we can bear. We have that promise. We will not break; we will not fail unless we give up. That is the only failure we can have in our lives. All bets are off if we give up. We can be successful as long as we continue. Even if we have fleeting moments of giving up, we can pick ourselves up, dust ourselves off, and return to it.

I had no peace as long as I was not in submission to the will of G-d. I had no peace as long as I tried to do things my way. I had no peace when I avoided asking G-d what He wanted for me. I had no peace as long as I only sought counsel from others to see what they thought I'd be good at.

There is no peace apart from serving the One who made us. This does not mean that everyone is destined to preach, teach, or otherwise be in full-time ministry, but everyone has a specific job that G-d has destined them for.

There are goers, and there are senders. For some, that means mentoring children. We need firefighters, politicians, doctors, teachers, ditch diggers, construction workers, pilots, you name it. G-d has a very specific job in mind for you. You may miss it unless you spend time in His Word and in prayer, seeking His will for your life. Missing the boat leads to a life of bitter frustration and unnecessary agony.

Seeking leads to answers…Submission to the answer leads to peace.

In my life, there was a specific period of disobedience and running from my destiny. Fear caused me to avoid my purpose. Sixteen years of my life were lost. G-d tells us He will restore the years, but how much greater would it have been to have submitted early and not need the restoration? How many souls were lost because of my disobedience? Someday, I will have the answer, and I know it will be horrible. I trust that the blood will cover my multitude of sins. "Woulda," "coulda," "shoulda." Avoid these three silly, life-sucking words at all costs.

Today, I have a newfound peace. I am not sure I can accurately describe exactly how I feel, but I will try. Finally, knowing and having confirmation that G-d has a specific plan for me and having it laid out before me, at least the outline, is an amazing gift. What a wonderful thing to know that your life has purpose and meaning! To have direction in my life is worth more than I could express.

There is still a bit of anticipation about my future. Many how's, why's, and when's are still left to be answered. I can, however, know that my life will count for something. I know that I have a specific ministry calling to fulfill. I know that G-d will lead me each step of the way. I know now that I will listen and follow. I know my days of avoiding and fearing my destiny are over.

It is a bit funny how I was so afraid of the call. I avoided it like you couldn't believe it, but now the fear is gone since I have submitted to that very call. I won't lie—there are some aspects of ministry that are a bit sobering and a bit big for me to swallow right now. Overall, such a sense of peace has enveloped me since I decided to serve Christ that words just cannot fully express.

It is almost akin to something I went through during the cancer experience of my life. There came such a fear and unsettledness in my spirit from the moment I was diagnosed with cancer. That fear persisted for the duration of the treatments. It was a scary time even though there were times when I hoped and believed I would survive; I felt that G-d wasn't done with me yet.

The day the doctors told me the cancer was in remission and that I could go home and stop treatments, there came such a feeling of relief. It didn't just trickle in; it rushed in like a mighty flood, a torrent. Yes, I knew there would be a time when uncertainty would still have some place in my life. I knew there would be monthly testing and monitoring, but those were potential troubles for another day. For this day in my life, there was no more cancer. That brought a sweeping flood of emotions- happiness, joy, and relief, just to name a few. Peace had come.

I had persevered through the dark time and entered a place of light. I left frustration and fear and entered into peace.

Hopefully, this begins to relay to you how it feels to acquire the peace that comes from being in a place of submission to the Will of G-d. I know that there are many troubles for the righteous. I also know that my G-d will carry me through. Look what He has already done for me! G-d is no respecter of persons; what he has done for me, He will also do for you. Ask Him.

Submission was accomplished in an instant, which doctor visits, medications, and worrying couldn't take away. Become a student of the Word. Immerse yourself in Scripture and in prayer. Surround yourself with G-dly men and women. Find a mentor in Yeshua. Make the will of G-d and His plan your priority, and sit back and get ready for an awesome, miraculous display of His love, grace, and favor in your life.

The antithesis of peace is frustration. The lack of peace kills. Don't believe me? Do a Google search on frustration or stress related to your health. There is a cascade of ill effects that come from negative feelings of anger, frustration, hopelessness, anxiety, etc. These emotions cause the release of certain stress hormones. These hormones can cause, among other reactions, inflammation. Systemic inflammation can result in so many different maladies it is ridiculous. These sicknesses include but are not limited to, heart disease and cancer.

Do you want good health? Do you desire a long life? Do you want the life you have to be a quality life? Do you want a blessed life? If so, then you must acquire peace.

Peace is essential to your body's ability to function the way G-d ordained it to function. The lack of peace can kill you if you allow it to do so.

Take charge of your life. The way to take charge and gain your life is to lose it. To lose it means to yield it to the L-rd or L-rds.

I have become thoroughly convinced that the greatest enemy in the battle for our peace is ourselves. There is no one person, and there is no enemy who can do to us what we can, and too often do, to ourselves. Nobody can affect our peace or steal our peace unless we allow it.

You will never let peace go once you get the full revelation of what having it in your life is worth. I titled this chapter "The Battle for Peace." The truth in that statement is staggering. Peace does not just happen. Peace does not come without a price. There is a war for our souls. One battlefield in that war is the mind. One of the greatest strongholds of the enemy can take is our peace. I will not go so far as to say that once you have peace, it will be yours forever. Like everything in life, peace comes and stays by process. Peace is achieved, but it can also be lost.

Understanding The Road Blocks

Part III

The Persuasion of Perseverance

CHAPTER NINE

Water is one of the most amazing substances on the planet. It comprises one part of oxygen combined with two parts of hydrogen. It is quite simple while at the same time altogether amazing. Water is transformable, too. Water is a liquid in its natural state. It becomes steam, or a gaseous vapor, above the boiling point. You get ice, a solid, if the temperature of water dips below freezing.

There is no life as we know it without water. Everything that lives on a cellular level contains water. Water is contained within a cell, known as plasma, and outside the cell. Each cell floats in water, known as interstitial or intercellular fluid. All living things take in water and give it off.

Men have studied and learned to master water throughout history. We have learned exactly how important it is for our health. We have learned the difference between healthy and unhealthy water. We have learned to harvest food and other riches from the seas, rivers, and lakes. Man has learned how to travel on water in boats. We use water to transport ourselves and the products of industry. Sadly, we have even learned how to exploit it for the purposes of war by using early warships and then graduating to the mighty and massive aircraft carriers the world knows today. We make war on top of the water, and we have even designed stealthy submarines with the power to devastate nations that patrol the deep.

Water itself is incredibly powerful. It can be as gentle as the morning dew as it covers the plains, but it can also destroy entire communities when floods come and oceans roar.

One of man's most difficult challenges has been to tame water's awesome power. Paddle houses along rivers have generated power for grinding corn and wheat. Today, massive dams have been constructed to redirect mighty rivers, create reservoirs, and produce unfathomable amounts of energy to power great cities.

Dams are some of man's most impressive architectural and engineering accomplishments. They boggle the mind with their scope and construction. They have served as useful tools that man seemingly could not live without. There is a dark side to dams. When a dam is correctly built and functioning, it is a marvelous wonder; however, when dams fail, they can demolish entire communities that they were intended to protect.

In the spiritual sense, we also have dams. They are every bit as dangerous and destructive in the spiritual as natural dams can be when they fail. Contrary to the natural, there are no good purposes for spiritual dams.

It is fairly common to hear people talk about "walls" that others put up in personal relationships. These walls, or dams, are usually erected to protect the builder and maintainer of the wall. The wall is constructed to keep something out or keep something in. Usually, it is to keep things out.

We tend to build walls to keep others at a safe distance when we suffer emotional injuries. We figure we can avoid being hurt in a similar fashion the next time if we don't allow someone the same access as those who have hurt us in the past.

While dams may be helpful to us in the short term, there is normally no long-term benefit. They only tend to harm us further by rendering us emotionally impotent. We are quarantining our feelings and not allowing people ever to get close us; we only harm ourselves. We keep ourselves from potentially satisfying relationships and situations. We limit our emotional and spiritual growth and our potential to receive blessings from G-d and deep friendships with others.

I think most of us can easily comprehend the deleterious effects of emotional walls. The effects of putting up barriers between others and ourselves are readily seen and often tangible.

One of the most horrible aspects of building a spiritual dam is that you rarely, if ever, fully comprehend the devastation and harm that it brings into your life. People will find out on the other side of eternity, but then it will be too late to change or reverse the harm.

The building blocks of spiritual dams are resistance and disobedience. I have been a saved, born-again Christian for nearly nineteen years. I spent approximately sixteen of those years building a spiritual super-dam to one degree or another. I am sure that if this super dam could be built in the natural, it would rival any dam physically created by any individual, corporation, or nation in the history of man.

You lay the foundation for a spiritual dam when you know G-d's will and run from it. Regardless of the reasons why we avoid doing the will of the Father, the results are always the same. Just look at Jonah. My reason for running from G-d was more out of fear than anything else. Dumb!

I've heard it taught that hesitation is disobedience. That thought resonated in my mind and spirit. It was a startling revelation to me. I used to think that as long as I got there eventually, then I was okay. The truth and reality is that if G-d tells me to move, He probably means NOW! If I fail to move, I'm guilty of disobeying the L-rd.

These acts of disobedience represent bricks that are used to build the dam. Dams hold back water from flowing in a particular direction in the natural. Spiritual dams do not halt or redirect the flow of water but the blessings of G-d. Every time I disobey my G-d, I further the construction of a structure that limits the flow of blessings into my life or simply turns them away altogether, possibly redirecting them to someone else.

Perseverance applies to dams in two ways. Negatively, we labor in the building up of that which chokes off the very supply we need most in our life when we press on and continually defy the will of G-d in our lives. Likewise, the recognition of the dams in our lives will hopefully birth repentance inside of us and the decision to persevere in seeking G-d out. The bricks will fall when we press on to hear G-d's voice, ask Him to reveal in us all the hidden bricks we have laid throughout our lives, repent, and strive to change. The integrity of the whole structure is in jeopardy, and it will eventually fall. The falling down of the dam will bring about an enormous release of power and energy.

In the natural, a dam will release destructive force if it fails. If the dam is great enough, this force will level whatever is in its path.

In the spiritual, the collapse of a dam releases an even greater force—the force and power of the Holy Spirit. In this sense, the destructive power is limited solely to the bad things in our lives that held the flow of the Spirit back in the first place. It is actually a constructive force for everything else in our lives related to the sudden release of the Spirit.

The destructive potential is obvious. The constructive force may look a bit like this. Imagine that at least part of the flood waters you are holding back are the floods of physical healing. This, in part, was true in my case. I have longed for healing of my eyesight my entire life. Ever since I was old enough to understand that I was different, I wanted to be healed completely in order to be the same as everyone else. My parents searched for a cure. They prayed often to G-d for my healing. Many others labored in prayer; they hoped and believed for a miracle to come. So many people labored in vain for some thirty-six years. I believe that no matter how much prayer was offered up, the healing was destined to remain held back.

How is that, you say? Doesn't the Bible tell us that healing was provided for on the cross? Isn't it already done? Aren't we to believe that it is already here and that all we have to do is believe in order to receive?

You must remember this: The Word of G-d says to "seek ye first the Kingdom of G-d and His righteousness, and all these things will be added unto you." The emphasis here is on the word "first." I'll take the statement of hesitation equaling disobedience a step further. I now wholeheartedly believe that if we don't first seek G-d in all things, we are, by default, living in a state of disobedience.

It is true that some blessings will still enter our lives. The rain falls on the just and the unjust alike. The law of sowing and reaping still works. Even an unrighteous man can sow seeds and reap a harvest. It is a law of G-d. However, we must walk in obedience to G-d to unlock the door to specific blessings, such as healing and to actually receive what has been provided. There must also be an

78

acknowledgment that G-d tests us. Read the book of Job. I ran from the call of G-d for some sixteen years. Unbeknownst to me, I was laboring in the resistance of my miracle! The miracle that I had sought, along with so many others, began to materialize once I surrendered my life completely and began to truly put G-d first for the first time in my life.

To attempt to explain the joy and excitement I feel at this moment for what G-d is doing in my life would be an exercise in futility. There are no words to describe how I feel now. I am now seeing miracles of healing manifest before my very eyes- no pun intended. I am also seeing the hand of provision from Jehovah-Jirah in new and more powerful ways.

The verse's writer about seeking the Kingdom was so wonderfully accurate. G-d's Word is true. G-d is not a man that He should lie. If G-d said it, and we do what He says, then the promised blessing must come tied to that particular act of obedience. We must remember that G-d also doesn't always answer in the way we expect. He is Sovereign. He sees the past, present, and future of every action. Living a lifestyle of obedience will put us on a straight and narrow path and will prevent dams from ever forming.

Consider the verse of Scripture, "…when the enemy comes in like a flood, the Spirit of G-d will lift up a standard against him" Isaiah 59:19. I cannot take credit for this following explanation, and I do not recall what preacher I heard suggest this, but I find it powerful. I am also not convinced that I, or anyone else, should advocate for any grammatical correction, but just examine a beautiful picture worth considering. In the accepted version, the comma is placed after the word flood. This implies that the enemy swarms in to attack and overtakes us. This is a bit of a scary image. When that attack comes, it simply states that the Spirit of G-d will come to our aid. However, if we were to move that comma back to just one word, it would change the whole picture dramatically. See for yourself. "When the enemy comes in, like a flood the Spirit of G-d lifts up a standard against him." In this comma placement, G-d swarms in with great power and overwhelming authority. It takes the picture of power away from the enemy and places it squarely with the L-rd. It also serves to illustrate my point about dams further. Picture, if you will, that we repent of our disobedience, which has built the dam that holds back blessings of all sorts. Once that barrier is removed, the Spirit of G-d moves in like a flood.

This is where I currently am in my life. The barrier has been removed. The dam has burst. The levees have failed, and I am now experiencing a flood of a different kind. I have had plenty of experience with disastrous spiritual floods in my life. Now, I am, for the first time, experiencing a spiritual flood that is not terribly unlike the magnitude of the flood of Noah's day.

The breakthrough of healing in my life alone has been worth the transformation necessary to break down the dam. In addition to that, there are other "good floods" that have started to roll in. Walking into my purpose in life is so satisfying to me. Seeing financial blessings come is miraculous as well. The very fact that this book is now "flowing" out of e has long been a dream of mine, and now it is coming to fruition.

I beg of you, for your own sake and for the sake of those you love, examine your spiritual life. Seek out the bricks that may have built a dam in your life. Ask G-d to help reveal even the hidden bricks below the waterline. G-d will be more than happy to show you what is blocking your path in order that you may remove them from your life. It really is G-d's will to bless us as rightful heirs through His Son Jesus.

An amazing thing about G-d is that even when we break covenant with Him, He remains faithful and still desires a relationship with us.

Sowing Perseverance

CHAPTER TEN

Monday morning, like all the rest of the week, the alarm sounds at 4:30 a.m. The man rises without hesitation, wipes the sleep from his eyes, and gets washed and ready for the day. Next, he has a good breakfast; the day will be long and difficult, and he knows to get fueled up right. Once breakfast is complete, he kisses his wife and children and heads out to the fields. As sure as the sun rises in the east, he has been faithfully working the ground.

Jim is a farmer, just like his father and grandfather before him. Springtime comes, and Jim sows seed in the field. In one section, he plants corn. He plants wheat in another, and in another, he plants lettuce. He tends the fields all summer long. He labors under sweltering heat. Jim battles weeds, pests, and other animals that would destroy his crops. Jim has invested large amounts of money in elaborate irrigation systems so that he will not lose his crops when the summer rains fail and drought comes. The summer is long and slow to pass, but Jim presses onward.

The life of a farmer is tough. The process is long and arduous. Patience must reign until the fall harvest time comes when Jim can reap his crops and sell them at the market to support his family.

How does he do it? Why does he do it? Surely, there are easier ways to support his family.

The reason is expectancy. The farmer knows and believes from experience the law of sowing and reaping. It is not a theory, nor is it a hope or even a fantasy. It is the law. It is a settled law, at that. There is no jury out deliberating the facts. No Supreme Court Justice in any jurisdiction can overturn it; this law stands eternal. The farmer knows that whatever he sows, he will also reap. According to Genesis, everything sown after its own kind will be reaped after its own kind. When the farmer plants wheat, undoubtedly, he will reap wheat. He will not plant apple seeds hoping for corn if corn is the desired crop. Corn begets corn. There is no way around it. It is what it is. Sowing the seed is not enough, though. There is much labor involved. The farmer must water, weed, prune, and fertilize. Why do all that labor? It is in the expectancy. The farmer fully expects and believes that all this hard work will pay off. At the appointed time of the season, he sows. Also, at yet another appointed time, he will reap the fruits of his labor. Expectancy fuels perseverance.

In this example, the farmer would never be so crazy as to persevere through the long, hot summer, toiling in the fields, if he did not first expect the harvest. That expectation keeps him going. When times get tough, the drought comes to his fields, and pestilence attacks, he focuses on the reward: his precious harvest.

Enough about farmers; let's apply this to our own daily lives. In my life experience, I can look back and now see the fruit of my expectations- good and bad. I had hope when I was dealing with cancer. That hope was that I would live and not die. This was quite a simple yet powerful hope. Let's face it: when you get that kind of diagnosis, you don't care what you have to lose Let the surgeons take out whatever they think necessary in order that I may live. The goal at that point is to extend and save your life.

If my seed of thought were that I was going to die, then I probably wouldn't be here today. Death would be the expectancy that came from the seed of doubt. There is no getting around it. I don't care how good my doctors were; if I expected that I would die, then die, I would.

For me, death was not an option! So, I planted seeds of life in my mind. I counseled with positive people. I read and listened to the positive Word of G-d. I fed my mind with thoughts of conquering this disease. I held the vision in my mind of cancer cells dying and healthy cells taking over. I watered the seeds of life that I planted in the soil of my mind. I held onto the expectancy of the coming miraculous day when I would walk out of that hospital for the last time. I expected to harvest life.

On the other side of the coin, there have been times when I found myself heading into a situation where I felt inadequate. I thought there was no way I could do that thing. Those were seeds of doubt and failure that I planted within myself, or at least allowed to be planted, which Satan was glad to promote. He does come to steal and destroy; don't forget. I worried about the situation. I failed to trust the L-rd, my G-d. Through my fear, I gave credence to the enemy instead of having faith in the supplier of all my needs. Those actions served to water and fertilize my fears. As Job himself said, "The very thing I feared has happened to me." The harvest came. It was not good.

Seed is seed. Whether it is good seed or bad seed, seed will produce after its own kind. In this case, I got that which I expected to get. Failure!

Praise G-d that we sometimes experience failure. We don't thank G-d for failure or problems for their own sake, but rather, we know that problems and tests that we go through position us for our next season. Even when I failed, I gained. At that particular moment, though, it might not have seemed true. The reality is that even failure brings experience. Even bad experiences can produce good lessons learned.

The law of sowing and reaping really changes you once you grasp it. It changes how you think, what you say, and how you act. We can't help but persevere when we have proper seed and proper expectancy. There really is no secret greater or deeper than that. Please get this point if there is nothing else that you can glean from this book. If you want to know the secret to persevere when everyone else around you quits, remember it is in the expectancy. That which you expect to happen will.

Currently, I am in one of the greatest battles of my life. This time, the battle is not for my life itself, as it was in the past. This time, I am in a battle for my sight. I sometimes have to battle to take back my mind, regain my thoughts, and refocus my energy. I persevere not because of what I have seen but because of what I expect. What I see now is the proof of my expectancy; therefore, my expectancy is what I continue to hold on to. No matter what happens in the natural, my expectancy is in the supernatural. I know in my heart of heart that eventually, the supernatural will overtake the natural, and that will be my new reality. To put it simply, what I want will become what I have. What I have will never become what I want. I will not give into the "settle for less" mentality. Sometimes, I would think that maybe this is my thorn in the flesh. Maybe I should just accept it and move on, but I refused to allow that thinking to continue in my life. I expect a full recovery of my sight. Why? It is promised in the Word of G-d. I know you must have, at one time or another, heard the saying, "G-d said it, I believe it, and that settles it." That is pretty much my mantra in life.

We need to get to a point in our lives where we really are like little children when it comes to faith. Just think of a little child for a moment. A child will believe pretty much anything you tell them. Tell them about the boogie man, and he or she will believe. Tell a little boy that if he touches a girl he will get cooties, and he believes and says, "Yuck!" Faith comes by hearing and hearing by the Word. I believe the Bible when I read that Jesus healed the blind. There is no doubt, no questioning, and no room for anything but trust. G-d said it, I believe it, and that settles it. When I read in the Word that Jehovah-Jirah is my provider, and He will supply all my needs according to His riches in Glory, I believe it! The Word is the seed, and G-d's Word will not return void. It must bring a harvest.

We will see miracles of all types in our lives if we can get to a place where we are like little children. Why? Belief and trust in the Word (the seed) produce expectancy (the fuel for perseverance). Remember, Romans tells us that suffering produces perseverance, perseverance produces character, and character produces hope. And hope never disappoints.

Expectancy is a part of our daily lives. It is truth whether or not we recognize it. We just need to figure out where we place our daily expectancy. Are we expecting to fail, or are we expecting to succeed? Are we expecting the miraculous or to be defeated? Do we expect the promotion at work, or do we expect we will be passed over by someone more experienced? Do we wake up and say, "Oh, no, it's Monday!" Or do we say, "YES! It's Monday- the start of a new week of opportunities!" There is an amazing power in whatever we expect. There is power in the perseverance it produces or fuels. The challenge for us is first to realize the truth in that statement. Secondly, we need to understand how it works, and finally, we have to apply it.

Happy times are ahead. Why? How do I know? Because I expect it! I fully expect that there will be a need to write a new book once this one is complete. Why? The answer is that I will need to share the wonders of the completed miracles of my healing. My eyes are healed in Christ Jesus. It was provided for on the cross. Jesus said, 'It is finished." I believe it. That settles it. There is a coming day when the healing will have no choice but to manifest in my life in completion.

I will gladly share that with you so you can see the process for yourself. I have plenty of documentation relating to the disease's presence. I can document the state of the disease from leading doctors and hospitals. There is no doubt as to the amount of damage that is done. Therefore, there will be no room for doubt as to the magnitude of the restorative and healing miracle the L-rd G-d, my Healer, will have performed in me. This will be my future testimony to the world.

What would your book read? What are you suffering from? What areas of your life are you lacking? What do you hope for? What is your level of faith? We all have a measure of faith. Even the tiniest of seeds will produce a harvest. Get in the Word of G-d; water and fertilize your faith. Don't allow yourself to entertain doubt. Focus on what you want. Sow seeds of faith. Sow financial seeds, and tell G-d what the seed represents; He will honor it.

Then, fuel your perseverance. Expect your miracle. Whatever it is, expect your miracle to come. It is on the way. I heard a preacher ask the age-old question, "Which came first, the chicken or the egg?" The answer to that question is the chicken came first. How can the harvest come before the seed? G-d put the chicken here with the seed already in it.

I did not benefit from that analogy through most of my tribulations. If I had, I would like to believe that I would be light years ahead of where I am today. The good news is that today, I have it, so my tomorrows will be light years ahead of where they might have been.

Igniting The Fire

CHAPTER ELEVEN

"Go and make disciples of all nations…"
Matthew 28:29

You and I are in a wonderful and unique position. We are positioned to take the gospel to the world, one person at a time. How is that you ask? I pray that what I have shared about my life in this book will do a couple things. First, I'm hoping that my life will be a living illustration of the above verse from Ecclesiastes. We do not go through anything that is truly unique. We all go through the same things. Each of us may experience something different than others; however, the fact remains true that whatever it is, it is common in the big picture. Secondly, I am hoping to empower you with the knowledge I have gained through my experiences. I hope that when you look at your own troubles through the perspective that I have shared, it will cause you to rise above your circumstances. I hope that this message will inspire you to persevere and grow through your personal trials. I sincerely trust that this new growth will lead you to a better understanding of why bad things happen to good people and these events are actually preparing us for greatness. Lastly, I hope that in some way, I can inspire you to share both what you have learned here and the challenges you have faced in your own life with others. I hope this book, coupled with your faith and experience, will cause you to share the love and wonderfulness of the L-rd Jesus Christ with others.

We are all given a measure of faith. My faith has recently been stirred to a whole new level. I never realized that everything I needed was available to me and that I had the power and authority to get it through G-d.

I have been stirred in my faith to pass that along to as many as possible. I intend to set fire (figuratively speaking) to everyone I encounter through this, future books, and every preaching opportunity I get. I have hope that, in some way, I will ignite a new fire of faith, perseverance, and character throughout the body of Christ. In turn, as the torch of renewed and inspired faith is passed from me to you, I hope that you will continue to pass it along as well.

I am no expert in the field, but I believe that one thing the worldwide body of Christ can use is a giant dose of perseverance. There are too many who are content living life right where they are. When dealt a bit with bad news in life, there are too many who tend to wallow in self-pity and impotence for far too long. There are great men of G-d who preach from pulpits in this country, but what we need now are men and women willing to get up off the pews and put their faith in action. We need more people to be doers of the Word of G-d and not hearers only. We are warned that faith without works is dead. We need the spirit within each of us to be ignited and set on fire for the things of the Almighty, Living G-d. This world needs more men and women willing to share the gospel and take their walk with Christ to the next level. There is no more room or time for sedentary Christianity. Wake up, O Church of the Living G-d!

I know that what I believe to be true is true. I know it because although I had spent time pushing through each life hardship, I remained within my own little box. I stayed within my comfort zone. While I was growing and getting stronger as an individual, I wasn't doing much of anything for the world at large. I had greatness within me, as do you. Greatness serves no purpose if we keep it bottled up inside of us. We have to rise above our mortal circumstances and look beyond to the eternal consequences of our lives.

Sometimes, we are scared into inaction when we look at the big picture. Christ gave us the Great Commission, which is to preach the gospel to the entire world. Wow, what an awesome responsibility! What a huge task! When we focus on the large picture laid out before us, sometimes the smaller, more attainable tasks that are right under our noses are overlooked. The thought of winning the world to Christ is unfathomable, but can you imagine winning one person to Christ? Can you imagine just sharing your own personal testimony with someone? It is not our job to get people saved. It is our job to be a witness for Yeshua. The Holy Spirit has the responsibility to convict. G-d's job is to judge; our job is to love. To love is simply to share.

Simple, isn't it? Any large task is usually easy to get done when you break it down to its most basic component. The sharing of the gospel is no different.

I do not point a finger at anyone. I am not talking down to anyone in this matter. I am as guilty as the next person. I am sharing this chapter because I believe it is what G-d wants me to do. Also, I used to keep my faith neatly tucked away so as not to disturb or offend anyone. Now, I have finally surrendered my life to Christ. Those who keep their lives will lose them. Those who lay down their lives will gain them.

I'm newly on the path to doing my part in the Great Commission. I am simply sounding the shofar and asking the question, "Who will come with me?"

Start by sharing what G-d has done for you. Some will ask, "What if I haven't had any major things to overcome in my life?" I say to them, "Are you saved?" If yes, then that is all the testimony you will ever need. Just being saved from eternal loss and condemnation in an eternal hell is reason enough to get excited and share with others. Whatever your story is, share it. Share this book with someone you love or someone you work with. Sow it into their lives. If it has done anything to help you or change you in any way, assume it will help them as well. Don't make the mistake I made for so many years. Don't keep your faith under wraps. Let it out!

Additionally, recognize that time is short. You don't need to spend too much time in front of the evening news and reading of the books of prophecy to understand that we are dangerously close to the end. The end of the dispensation of grace is about to close. The stage is set for the beginning of the "end times" events…the rapture of the church, Armageddon, and the millennial reign.

If not now, when? Isn't it time to get going? Start or increase the sharing of your testimony. Don't get caught unprepared. Share! Share! Share!!

The Bottom Line

Part IV

The Promotion of Perseverance

CHAPTER TWELVE

I have covered a lot of ground in a short time. I tried to keep the chapters and the book, in general short and manageable. There are so many more details that could be shared on each individual topic but time and practicality don't allow.

Please try to get into your mind and spirit some basic thoughts:

1. Troubles are allowed to help us grow, not punish us.
2. All things do indeed work together for good, for those who love the L-rd!
3. Even our mistakes, failures, and shortcomings should be looked at with thanksgiving – not for the sake of the experience, but for the good that G-d will bring forth from them.
4. We all have greatness within us because we are created in G-d's

image, and His Holy Spirit resides in us.

5. We are called. Serve G-d with all that is within you.
6. There are certain immutable truths, or laws, in life. They will work for you if applied. For example, sowing and reaping etc.
7. Time is short! Act Now!

I am no legal authority by any means. However, my limited understanding of the law leads me to draw a few conclusions. There are certain documents that are intended to dictate behavior and guarantee rights and responsibilities. For example, the Constitution of the United States guarantees its citizens certain "inalienable rights." The document known as the Holy Bible also guarantees the children of G-d certain things.

The Bible tells us that we are children of the King. We are joint heirs with Christ. We are the seed of Abraham. We are His heirs. Being an heir indicates a legal right to an estate. Understand that the rights we have as heirs are plentiful. We have the right to health, prosperity, etc.

There are also responsibilities. We rarely, if ever, get rights regarding anything without having added responsibilities. Unfortunately, people are quick to claim their rights but equally quick to avoid or flat-out deny their responsibilities.

We have a responsibility to persevere through our adversities. We have a responsibility not to remain a baby feeding on milk but to grow and eat the meat of the Gospel. We have the responsibility to share and spread the Besorah—Hebrew for the Good News of the Gospel of Jesus Christ.

There is nothing terribly unique or impressive about Jeff Grillo. I am one of approximately six billion people residing on planet Earth. I am a mere grain of sand in the midst of a vast desert. However, the difference between someone being obscure and blending in with the crowds and someone willing to stand out is this: Surrender. Plain and simple. The surrender of our wills for the will of G-d is the difference. You never in a million years would have heard about me had I not submitted to the will of G-d, but because of the surrender, through the amazing works of the Father, I trust that many will know my name. Not for my glory or benefit, but for the Glory of Jesus Christ, my L-rd and Savior.

What's in It for Me?

CHAPTER THIRTEEN

So, exactly what is in it for you? Perhaps a better question would be, what isn't in it for you? The old Steven Curtis Chapman son, "Great Adventure," pretty much sums it up! Life is a great adventure, or at least it can be. This is a life like no other…this is the great adventure!

Many people have said that life is a journey. Submission and obedience to G-d's will and plan for your life is equal to embarking on a great adventure. Apart from G-d and His supreme will, life is more of a hopeless wandering. It can be a nomadic crisscrossing of a barren landscape. We can feel hopeless, empty, and unsatisfied without knowing G-d's purpose in our lives. People think wrongly that to become a Christian, or to live a Christian lifestyle is to live a life full of things that must be given up. The only things I gave up were hopelessness, worthlessness, and the sense of being lost.

What you get out of a Christian life is so much more than you could ever even hope for. You get purpose, destiny, hope, wisdom, knowledge, character, and a host of other benefits too numerous to mention. If you submit to and follow the L-rd completely, you also get peace in your spirit. The most obvious and important benefit of all is eternal life. That is prosperity! Need I say more? Probably not, but for those who still need more, here I go…

Assuming you have accepted Christ, and I hope that you have, you will one day stand before G-d in Heaven. Even the righteous must be judged. For Christians, this is not the same judgment that the non-believer faces. This is the judgment where our works for the Kingdom are judged before the L-rd. All the "wood, hay, and stubble" will be burned up. Only things of lasting, eternal value will be left. These are jewels. We will be left with crowns, jewels, precious metals, and the like. The Bible tells us that we will lay it all down at the feet of Jesus. This is our way of telling Him we are not worthy but that He alone is worthy.

I don't know about you, but that is one party I don't want to go to empty-handed! Can you imagine being left with ashes after all your works are burned up? Is that what you want to present to the L-rd? That's not what I want to give Him, that's for sure!

In addition to gaining insight, perspective, and hope, you will gain the tools to store up wealth and treasures in heaven for yourself.

Salvation is a gift—a free gift, not of works. Salvation is the only freebie promised in the Bible. Everything else you must earn. Submission to His will and the perseverance you endure through whatever may come your way will get you to the prize that He has preordained for you.

I hope you are like me and desire to hear the Father tell you one day, "Well done, my good and faithful servant." That is what I want to hear most of all when I see Him.

Serve the L-rd, your G-d, with all your heart. Seek Him first, and have no other gods before Him. Surrender your life to gain it.

In reality, by walking in obedience to G-d, you have nothing at all to lose but every good thing to gain.

If you need more than that…I'm not sure you really read this book.

Take Action!

CHAPTER FOURTEEN

Well, there you have it. Hopefully you've been inspired and challenged by my true life stories. I hope that your life has been touched and that you are moved to live differently.

Now comes the hard part…getting up and getting something done for the L-rd! It's time to take action in your life. Recognize that you are not living in some hopeless situation that nobody else can understand. Realize that you have the tools you need to get and stay connected to the Spirit of G-d. You know how to position yourself for greatness. Now, all you have to do is make the decision!

How do I take action? Just decide to walk in faith. Every day, you will wake up and be faced with questions. Should I go to church today? Should I serve here or there? Should I read the Word? We have to make countless decisions regarding our spiritual walk every day. We can struggle and wrestle with many daily decisions, or we can make one decision. I suggest you make the one.

Life will be ridiculously difficult if you live according to a multitude of decisions. Life will be so much easier if you make one decision. Do you know what that one decision is? Here it is: decide once and for all that you will always serve the L-rd.

Once that decision is made, guess what? Everything is decided! Think of any questions you could have. Should I go to church or go to the game? I will serve the L-rd. Should I read the Bible, take a nap, go to the store, or spend time with my friends? I will serve the L-rd. Should I volunteer for that ministry at church or be more social with people at work? I will serve the L-rd. you name it, it applies. Making that one decision will set you on the path to taking action in your daily life, enabling you to be more effective for the ministry of the Gospel. Taking action can take so many forms. Seek G-d and His will for your life. That is the only way to know exactly what you are to do. But know this: you are to do something! There should be no idle Christians!'

G-d isn't looking for men and women to warm the bench on Sunday. He's not looking for people to fill the church parking lot, so the pastor gets much credit for being the most popular church in town. G-d is looking for men and women of action. He wants people that will say, whatever the question, "Yes, L-rd!" He is looking for people who will say yes to the call and then act on it. We are to move towards His goals. We are to move towards His purpose.

Get involved. Take action. Share your testimony. Share the good news of Christ Jesus. Give to effectual ministries. Sow seeds! Be a tither. Be an active member of your local congregation. Do something; don't just warm a seat. Study. Be prepared and full of the Word. Give your time. Ask your pastor what he needs, and if possible, supply it. Whether it's time, talents, or something else. Find someone willing to mentor you. Be a mentor to someone younger in the faith than yourself. There are so many options; it is impossible to list all the ways we could be involved.

Not all are called to be missionaries, pastor churches, or host television or radio programs, but we are all still called to serve. Let G-d tell you in what capacity you are to serve. Just be obedient in whatever He tells you. Never despise humble beginnings. We ought to do the work of G-d that he has commanded.

Conclusion

The Final Word

I honestly hope you enjoyed reading this book as much as I enjoyed writing it. It took me a lot to share some of the things I did, but I know the Holy Spirit led me to do it. I trust that many who read it are forever changed by it. For those of you who thought you were getting a positive mental attitude book or a motivational speech in book form, surprise!

If you are not a Christian, I want to take this special moment to speak directly with you. Maybe you were inspired or touched by the power that was displayed in my life through perseverance. I hope and pray now that you realize it was not Jeff Grillo's power at all but rather the love and power of the Living G-d. If you felt the Holy Spirit tugging at your heart at any time, please don't keep the Spirit waiting. It is time to take action and begin your great adventure.

I am reminded of the Scripture that says, "no one is righteous, no not one." Other Scriptures tell us that "all have sinned and fallen short of the Glory of G-d." We are all lost, and we are all guilty of breaking His supreme law. We are separated from G-d eternally. That's the bad news. The good news is this: G-d has paid our debt in full. He gave His Son, Jesus Christ, as a sacrifice to pay for your sins. Jesus was crucified, died, and was buried for your sins and mine. He rose again on the third day and sits at the Father's right hand. He is our soon-returning King.

If you want to be spared from judgment and have a second chance at life, pray this prayer right now with me:

"Father, I acknowledge that I am a sinner. I have not kept all of your commands and am guilty and worthy of the penalty of enteral death. I understand that you made the perfect blood sacrifice by giving Your Son, Yeshua. Through His death, burial, and resurrection, it is now possible for me to have Him be my personal blood sacrifice, once and for all. Please forgive me and cleanse me of all my sins, transgressions, and iniquity through His atoning blood. Make me new in Your sight. I ask all this in the name of Your Son, Yeshua. Amen!"

If you prayed that prayer and meant it sincerely, I can assure you that you are indeed saved and now belong to G-d! What now? This is just the beginning step of a journey that will last the rest of your life. Get yourself a Bible and begin to read it. Pray before each time you read and ask G-d to teach you His ways as you read, and His Holy Spirit will help you.

Also, you need to plug into a community of believers and learn and grow with them. Pray G-d will show you the place He wants you to be connected. In the notes section at the end of this book, I will include some of my favorite Bible versions for you to check out. Some of them are online and FREE! If you want further assistance in finding a church home that teaches the Word of G-d the way it was originally taught by first-century believers, then email me (jeff@jeffgrillo.com), and I will help you locate a congregation in your area. Please contact me. I want to know that you have accepted your Savior so that I may pray for you.

Now, how does all this fit together? Your eternal soul is secure if you sincerely prayed to G-d. As for the here and now, it will prove to be your ultimate source of strength. It doesn't matter what obstacles you face; you will still have obstacles in all likelihood; now, you will walk through them with the understanding that you are not alone! The G-d that created you now resides in you! You can handle all things! Get involved. God bless you!

Epilogue

I want to take a brief moment to sincerely thank you for purchasing this book and reading it. I hope that it has encouraged, motivated, and inspired you.

Please feel free to contact me and share whatever is on your mind via email: jeff@jeffgrillo.com

Be certain to get your copy of my second book, *The Excuse Assassin*.

Thank you again!

Jeff Grillo

Made in the USA
Columbia, SC
03 September 2024

41541297R00061